Cabbages & Kings
A Kid's Guide To Tallinn, Estonia

Photography By John D. Weigand
Poetry By Penelope Dyan

Bellissima Publishing, LLC
Jamul, California
www.bellissimapublishing.com

copyright © 2011 by Penny D. Weigand & John D. Weigand

All rights reserved. No part of this book may be reproduced or transmitted in any form or by any means, electronic or mechanical, including photocopying, recording, or by any other means, or by any information or storage retrieval system, without permission from the publisher.

ISBN 978-1-61477-002-2
First Edition

"The time has come," the Walrus said,
"To talk of many things:
Of shoes--and ships--and sealing-wax--
Of cabbages--and kings--
And why the sea is boiling hot--
And whether pigs have wings."

The Walrus and The Carpenter
Lewis Carroll
From Through the Looking-Glass and What Alice Found There, 1872

Cabbages & Kings
Bellissima Publishing, LLC

Introduction

The first traces of human settlement found in Tallinn's city center by archeologists are about 5000 years old. The comb ceramic pottery found on the site dates to about 3000 BC and corded ware pottery c. 2500 BC. Then in 1154 a town called Qlwn (or Qalaven) was put on the world map of the Almoravid by the cartographer Muhammad al-Idrisi who described it as a small town like a large castle among the towns of Astlanda.

John D. Weigand and Penelope Dyan went to the town of Tallinn, Estonia and would agree the cartographer's description is very accurate when it comes to this town, because it is exactly like stepping into a castle province, and you can imagine it exactly as it once was, a place of cabbages and kings. This is a place for a child to fire up the imagination inside, to hear music, to eat candied almonds sold in little bags on the street, to watch archers with bows take aim at targets, and to walk among green paths, cobblestones and flowers.

Cabbages & Kings
Bellissima Publishing, LLC

Cabbages & Kings
A Kid's Guide To Tallinn, Estonia

Photography By John D. Weigand
Poetry By Penelope Dyan

There is a place called Tallinn,
Estonia, where time stands still,
where once a grand castle
stood tall on a hill.
As you enter Tallinn you see
the Fat Margaret Tower,
built to make castle enemies cower.

You walk through the lower town gate,
like a princess, prince or king.
Then you take time, you pause and wait
as you hear the church bells ring.

There's an antique shop.
And you look at the wares.
The people seem happy here,
and free of all cares.

On the way to the top of the hill,
you decide to look and shop.
You see the town square, touring kids,
and quite more than a lot.

There are colorful buildings
and the places to eat
look bright and cheerful
against the grey cobblestone street.

You see a little girl in a pink hat, one of the smallest of the small. She walks across the cobblestones towards the upper city wall.

You see things here
and you see things there.
Then you decide to leave
the main city square.

You walk down a narrow street.
Cobblestones fly beneath your feet.

There is a building of pink
and another gate.
You're almost to the top,
and you just CAN'T wait!

You walk through the gate arch
next to the wall.
The history of Tallinn
makes you feel small.

You see the Russian Cathedral,
golden images shine in the sun.
You are almost to the top,
the journey nearly done.

You get to the top wall.
Then you look down.
Below you see a beautiful town.
In your head you make up a story,
of kings and queens, of medieval glory.
You think about the glorious past.
Sadly, you realize NOTHING can last.
But every day begins anew.
And every day is made for you.
All of life is filled with glory.
YOUR life unfolds its very own story.

As back through the town you wend,
you realize everything has its own end.
You know the future belongs to you,
that your own dreams CAN come true.
That night you dream of good things,
of princes, of princesses,
of cabbages, of kings.

"O Oysters," said the Carpenter,
"You've had a pleasant run!
Shall we be trotting home again?'
But answer came there none--
And this was scarcely odd, because
They'd eaten every one.

The Walrus and The Carpenter
Lewis Carroll
From Through the Looking-Glass and What Alice Found There, 1872

www.ingramcontent.com/pod-product-compliance
Ingram Content Group UK Ltd.
Pitfield, Milton Keynes, MK11 3LW, UK
UKHW060136240426
12048UKWH00002B/59